Crochet Fingerless Gloves
10 Amazing Crochet Patterns

All photos used in this book, including the cover photo were made available under a Attribution 2.0 Generic (CC BY 2.0) and sourced from Flickr.

Table of content

Introduction 3
Chapter 1 – 5 Marvelous Crochet Patterns 4
Chapter 2 – Another 3 patterns 15
Chapter 3 – 2 Great and new patterns! 26
Chapter 4 – The Ideas Behind Crochet Patterns 30
Conclusion 33

Introduction

Even though itis frequently merely known as cashmere cashmere is actually a favorite kind of wool. The vast majority of this wool originates from Mongolia and it is extracted from the Cashmere Goat. Its soft materials characterize cashmere. Without being large like different wools, it offers efficiency and superb temperature. Cashmere fingerless gloves are light, smooth and extremely cozy.

Angora wool describes the Angora rabbit's outer hair coat. Angora is known for soft texture and its softness.

Its often found in sweaters and as yarn for sewing. Angora wool is favored by hobby individuals who like to make their very own fingerless wool gloves.

Merino is another kind of wool from Merino sheep. It is one of the wools because wonderful fibers. It highly popular in running clothing because the wool wicks moisture from the body preserving the wearer cool also during strenuous activity. Merino wool fingerless gloves are perfectly worthy of the active lifestyle.

Fleece is really a synthetic wool produced from Polyethylene terephthalate (DOG). Its a lighting and strong material supposed to substitute some wools. Fleece pullovers have not become undue to their delicate, light feel and heat. It creates superb fingerless gloves which can be cozy and comfortable. Fleece can also be a vegan option to wool.

When you can easily see, knit gloves that were fingerless could be made from the variety of diverse textiles, organic and man-made. This mobility accounts for the wide array of colorful types and styles. A pair of fingerless gloves is the great solution to exhibit your creative side therefore release and also have some fun!

Chapter 1 – 5 Marvelous Crochet Patterns

Crochet Openwork Hand warmers:

This Can Be A very simple routine, great for any crocheter who's able put their abilities to make use of creating a dress and to go beyond the granny square. Having said that, they're good looking enough any experienced crocheter could be very happy to wear them!

Terms:

ch = string

Dc = double crochet

hdc= half double crochet

sl st = slip stitch

sk = skip

Gauge: " 3dc, ch2 " twice * 5rows – 5 * 5,5cm

Size female

(any worsted weight wool)

Hook

Handwarmer's cuff:

Ch 35, sl st to make ring, mindful to not twist the ch.

Round 1: ch3, DC-in following 2 ch, ch1, sk 2ch ch1, sk 2ch*. Across stopping round with ch1 st in third ch og ask repeat from*. ch3.

ch3.

Round 3: ch3, 2dc in ch1 space, *3dc in subsequent space, ch1, ch1*. Repeat from * across, closing with ch1 st in third ch of beg. ch3.

Round 5: repeat round 3.

FROM HERE ON produce 2ch between each 3dc party in place of 1ch (which means that you make 5ch instead of 4ch at the start of every round 2).

Continue performing rows 2 and 3 before the position where you are going to make the thumb hole.(I Have produced an overall total of 11 lines from cuffis bottom to thumb hole), finishing with a row 3.

Thumb-hole:

Row 1: Sl st in 1 ch of ch2 place of prior round as well as in every ofthe 2 dc.

Ch3, 2dc in identical space, *ch2, 3dc in following space*.Repeat from * across until previous round's last space , 1dc in space, ch3, switch.

Beginner's Wrist Warmers

Another great beginner structure that looks excellent too! This couple is worked as being a flat rectangle, side-to-side. The end product is super-warm and cozy, along with a very different glance from your above.

For that cooler nights, listed here is a set of arm warms (fingerless gloves) to crochet. They're made to fit warm and keep your arm and arms exceedingly cozy while making your palms free to move. As a beginner level sample, you will crochet a rectangle that can fold around your supply. The part will likely then be attached closed, making a tiny pit to your flash. These wrist warmers are fast and easy to crochet! crochet starter arm warmers

Skill Level: starter crochet skill level

Finished Size: 3" (7.5 cm) extensive, 9 1/2" (24 cm) long – size small

Note: Arm warmer can also be altered using the directions inside the structure. Hand warmer should stretch to fit neatly.

Products:

Medium-Weight String (around 200 yards)

String Hook   crochet yarn size 4

Row 1: ch 41 (or a sequence that is along your desired wrist warmer from lower supply to palm of palm), sc in minute ch from catch as well as in each ch across: 40 sc

Line 2: ch 1, switch, sc in back trap just of every sc across: 40 sc

Repeat row 2, twenty-eight instances or beforehand warmer wraps comfortably around wrist, your hand and lower supply. Remember that the arm warmer should extend.

Use string needle to sew factors of hand warmer together making a 2" (5 cm) hole 1" (2.5 cm) from the end.

Puff Stitch Fingerless Gloves

Puff Stitch Fingerless Gloves by Olivia Kent, on My Favorite Points: the wrist cuff that is buttoned is indeed good, as well as I really like the entertaining texture of those! There are plenty of photographs here and that I think this routine looks very doable. She actually contains instructions in making them in custom shapes!

Everything You'll Need:

4.50 Crochet Hook

8ply wool of the choice

Wool hook

Scissors

Size:

You can make this for any dimension individual, only measure your hand

And make the ribbing that massive, plus 4cm.

Wrist Ribbing:

Create a Slipknot.

Strip 1- consider your crochet hook and force it in to the second string from land. Currently Single Crochet until end of strip.

Line 2- String 2 then press your crochet hook in to the second last single crochet. Continue to create single crochets until the row's end.

Row 3- Same as strip 2.

Line 4- and soon you reach the last 4 stitches, Do a similar as line 2. Crochet 2 chain stitches, skip to stitches and force crochet hook to the second last stitch of this line. Simple crochet last 2 stitches.

Strip 5 - 7- just like strip 2

Line 8- identical to row 4

Strip 9 - 12- just like strip 2

Note: Do a pair less lines in case you'd prefer to make a kid a smaller-size.

Now fasten it off.

Select 4 keys that you like, then sew 2 links on each arm ribbing should you buttoned up them where they would be.

Button the ribbing up.

Hand:

Line 1-Make a Slip-Knot. Getting your crochet hook, drive it through where both finishes of the wrist ribbing overlap. Crochet Simple Crochets all around the whole ribbing. Note make sure to push it through both levels to wherever the ribbing overlaps whenever your come.

Strip 2- Now once you've crocheted single crochets all around the ribbing it really is moment to start out crocheting Smoke Stitches! Note: This sample features a Smoke Stitch which can be a bit tough to spell out. I've a beneficial training that is movie below that needs to be very helpful.

Strip 3 - 4- Crochet a Puff Stitch Round 2, miss one stitch. Crochet a Puff Stitch, sequence 2, miss one stitch etc. next row you'll be crocheting your Smoke Stitches in to the room where you chained 2 around the past row. This helps produce that zigzag pattern.

Strip 5- This Can Be wherever you add the pit to your thumb. For each individual it's various, so you need to choose now where you need your thumb to become. Whenever you make it crochet a Puff Stitch, then crochet 3 string stitches (might need to ensure it is four for those who have massive thumbs) Then perform a double crochet into the next stitch, and create a puff stitch because same stitch.

Continue creating smoke stitches completely around. Note: If you're building a smaller-size do the thumb-hole alternatively as row 4.

Strip 6 - 8 - Repeat row 3. Note: Do one strip of smoke stitches to create a smaller-size.

Line 9 - 10- Single crochets entirely around.

Fasten off, and you are completed.

Twist Fingerless Glove Pattern

The prolonged arms are certain to preserve you comfortable and great too! The pattern includes every phase to be explained by tons of photographs, therefore this design can be made by you even though they seem intricate!

For this routine you'll want to be (or get) familiar with:

Blo=back loop

Post that is fpdc=front crochet

You should use any weight string with a slightly huge catch (and optionally the more expensive lift too for the the surface of the glove) for that string you're using. The larger crochet hooks help to keep it supple. Measure isn't crucial because you'll create you're able to only gauge the gloves against your palm and supply when you move or the gloves to fit. You will need afew measurements. The 2nd approach actually works best for me... plus I attempt them on at each step. Then you can obtain the appropriate rigidity/stretchiness feel. Keep in mind these gloves are very flexible so they can be made by you a little about the aspect that is modest, simply don't make sure they are too large.

Cuff- The cuff can be a basic 1:1 ribbing.

Ch (together with your smaller lift) before you achieve the around. Size from rating No 1 plus 1 more sequence. (I chained 19)

Strip 2: sc blo in every, ch 1, change

Row 3-?: Repeat line 2. Just how many lines you produce will soon be dependant on description Number 2 and No 3. It should fit around your wrist without gapping but be able to extend to across the top of one's palm (to help you obtain it on.) I'd 24 rows.

You will end up getting a square/rectangle-shaped item. ch 1, turn. For your body you'll work along the cuff's part

Body-

Line 1: In the ribbed cuff's medial side , sc across. it must be a factor of 5 although how many sc you will need is determined by your dimensions. You desire it to suit perfectly around your wrist but have the ability to stretch over the top of the palm in order to get it on. I had 25 sc total. Fold in half to begin working in the round and Join to sc of this row with sl st.

Strip 2: ch 3, create beginning perspective (dc in sc behind where you merely joined-view photographs below), sk 1, 3dc in next (cover) *Make twist (sk 2, dc, dc in 2nd skipped stitch), sk 1, 3dc in next* Replicate around, (5 twists and 5 covers complete)

In other words, for this line and each line after, you will be folding in each pose and performing a shell in the room before each cover.

Row 4: Repeat line 3 and soon you arrive at the row where you'd like to work your thumb hole. You might want to change to your lift that is bigger 1-2 rows before your thumb hole strip.

Thumb hole row: perform a new twist sew (like in row 3 and on: join with sl st around dc from row below, ch 3, fpdc around ch 3 of below strip) dc in area before subsequent shell, ch 6, sk the shell and the next twist, dc in space before following shell, *twist in next twist, shell in space before following shell* repeat about, join with sl st around the post of the very first dc

Next strip and until top: Repeat line 3, end, and sew the cuff up. Oh, and don't forget to make a different one for that other-hand!

V-Stitch Fingerless Gloves

V-Stitch Fingerless Gloves on Crafts by Sinjah, by Daphne Bekiari: in case you are quick on string – only 92 meters had a need to get this to match This Is Actually The routine that is ideal! I imagine you might produce a pair of these up very fast.

Yarn weight

Land: 4.5mm/U.S. G

Abbreviations

Ch: string

Sc: single crochet

Dc: double crochet

Sl st: slip stitch

FPHDC: Front-post half- double crochet

BPHDC: Back-article half- double crochet

Cuff

Ch 28, join with sl st, being cautious to not twist the Round,

Round 1: sc in most stitch around, Ch 1, join to ch 1 with sl st

Round 2: Ch 1, *FPHDC in subsequent sc, BPHDC in second sc, repeat from * about, join with sl st to ch1

Glove

Round 5: Ch 3, 2 DC-in same stitch, *skip 2 stitches, 3 dc in third stitch, replicate until there are only 2 stitches left, from * around, join to ch 2

Round 6: Sl st in middle power of dc cluster, ch 4, DC-in identical stitch, *dc in middle stitch of dc cluster, ch 1, DC-in same stitch, repeat from * around, join to 3rd ch of ch 4

Round 7: Sl st in ch replicate from * about, 1 space 2 DC-in same space, *3 DC-in next ch 1 space, join to ch 3

Round 8: Repeat Round 6

Flash house

Round 10: Repeat Round 6 until the last electricity cluster, skip the last power cluster, and join to 3rd string of ch 4 with sl st

Round 11: Repeat Round 7

Round 14: Ch 1, sc in every sew about, join to ch 1, fix down.

Optional: Flash

Join string at thumb beginning.

Round 1: Ch 1, *sc 2 sc in area of dc space created by Round 10 of pattern, in every stitch, replicate from * around thump room and sl st, join to ch 1

Round 2-3: Repeat Round 1.

Strategies for the sample being decreased by / that is growing:

-You need a numerous of three plus one for that beginning Round.

-For a larger palm, in Circular 10 of routine you might need to skip the last two dc clusters rather than the last one.

Chapter 2 – Another 3 patterns

Owl Mitts

yarn & thoughts:

About 100 yards of worsted weight wool.

In grape owls are blue sky dyed cotton in Thistle.

H land (or whatever measurement you have to fit your hand)

4 about half-inch round beans for eyes (optional)

Measure:

The gauge here is about 7 dc = 2inches to acquire a glove that fits a palm that's 7.5" around

the knuckles.

It should match perfectly around your hand, when you've worked the very first round.

Rather the right match by changing hooks, you take or can add a stitch or two on the hand area

of the hand, from the seam.

Guide:

ch: chain stitch

Dc crochet

Fpdc: post crochet that is front

Fptc: front post treble crochet

Pull through three loops, yarn over, and Round, string over and pull-through outstanding loops (this is

not the typical double crochet decrease, but I preferred just how that one formed the glove).

owl pattern lines:

The owls are made in a twelve stitch wide strip down the back by creating two

cables alongside. The three lines guidelines repeated essential to produce the owls.

OWL MIX: skip 4 stitches, 2 fptr, ch 2, reach in front of the trebles and fptr in all the 2

fpdcs you missed, miss 4 stitches, 2 fptr (to the far couple of fpdcis), ch 2, reach behind the

Trebles in each one of the 2 fpdcs you skipped, skip at night remaining cabling,

OWL 1: 2 fpdc, 2 DC-in ch space, 4 fpdc, 2dc in ch space, 2 fpdc

OWL 2: 2 fpdc, 2 dc, 4 fpdc, 2 dc, 2 fpdc

Note that the OWL CORNER strip can look really unpleasant till you've worked two or a row after it.

The point that makes cords function is the fact that you perform the stitches of the line out of order, and this is

The row that is accomplished by that.

Mitt:

String 30, without folding, slip stitch to hitch.

R1: ch 2 (matters as dc here and often) 29 dc around, sl to join. (30)

R2: ch 2, 15 dc, 2 fpdc, 8 dc, 2 fpdc, 2 dc, sl to join. (30)

2 dc, R3: ch 2 OWL CORNER, sl to join. (30)

R4. (30)

R5: ch 2, 10 dc skip 3 stitches, 2 dc, OWL 2, 2 dc, sl to hitch.

R6: ch 2, 10 dc, dc in each sequence (7), 2 dc, OWL CROSS, 2 dc, sl to affix. (34)

2 dc, r7: ch 2, 10 dc, dcr OWL INCH, sl to join. (33)

R8: ch 2, dcr, 8 dc, dcr, 6 dc, OWL 2, 2 dc, sl to affix. (31)

R9: ch 2, 8 dc 3 dc dc, OWL 2, 2 dc, sl to affix. (29)

R10: ch 2, 8 dc 4 dc 2 dc, sl to hitch. (28)

R11. (28)

R12- 15 sl to hitch. (28)

Second mitt:

Round 30, without twisting, slip stitch to hitch.

R1: ch 2 (counts as dc below and usually) 29 dc about, sl to join. (30)

15 dc, R2: ch 2 2fpdc, 8 dc, 2 fpdc, sl to participate. (30)

R3: ch 2, 2 dc 15 dc, sl to participate. (30)

R4: ch 2, 2 dc sl to hitch. (30)

10 dc, R5: ch 2, 2 dc, OWL 2, 2 dc, miss 3 stitches, ch 7, sl to affix.

R6: ch 2, 2 dc, OWL COMBINATION, 2 dc, dc in each string (7), 10 dc, sl to join. (34)

10 dc, r7: ch 2, 2 dc, OWL INCH, 7 dc, dcr, sl to affix. (33)

Dcr, R8: ch 2 OWL 2, 6 dc 8 dc, sl to affix. (31)

R9: ch 2, 2 dc, OWL 2, dc 3 dc 8 dc, sl to join. (29)

R10: ch 2, 2 dc 4 dc, dcr, 8 dc, sl to hitch. (28)

R11. (28)

R12-15: ch 2 sl to participate. (28)

Completing:

In the finger-beginning of each glove, opposite crochet around.

Weave in most finishes.

Recommended: sew a bead to the spaces inside the wires closest towards the hand starting as eyes. The beads

Described are half- round jet beads flattened.

Easy Victorian Shell Mitts

Aran weight wool.

Catch - H

Level Of Skill - Easy

Size - one-size fits. Nevertheless, you may make by crocheting 4 less the mitts smaller

Lines about the wrist ribbing. (4 lines = 2 lines of rib = 1 layer and 1 dc.) They can be sized by you

up by the addition of 4 lines of sc about the arm ribbing, therefore incorporating 2 lines of rib, one layer

And 1 DC-in the mitts' body. You will need to regulate your shell dc count appropriately in

The pattern's body.

Related Nailpolish - Elective. ::wink::

Routine stitches employed - 2 dc in room, Starting layer = Ch3 ch1.

Layer - 2 dc 2 dc in room that is same.

Measure - 3 covers/3 dc (in routine) = 4" 7 lines of shells = 4"

Finished size: 4" broad in lace part, 7 INCH/2" long, base of ribbing to top of lace.

ROUTINE:

Ch 10.

Note: For lines 1 through 22 in arm ribbing.

Change, Strip 1: Sc in ch from hook ch 1. 9 sc.

Lines 2 - 22: Sc in every sc across, ch 1, change.

Strip 23: Provide strip 1 to meet up corresponding stitches, strip 22. Sl st strip 1 and strip 22.

11 ridges created.

Split yarn. Change cuff inside out (therefore sl st advantage is inside) and change cuff therefore the ridges are

Operating vertically, connect with sl st within the aspect of the first sc in line 1.

Lace part:

Cuff, dc on cuff in aspect of 1st sc in strip, sk sc row, layer in next in aspect of sc

* replicate between *is 4 times more, Strip. Sk line conclusion, DC-in side of sc aspect, sl st in

ch 3. (based on the way you slide sewn the ends you may

Not need an entire sc row to place your last dc in. If you-can't miss AROW, simply put it within the

next line. No foul, no damage. Sincere - it surely wont really make a difference.)

At this point you have 6 /dc mixtures that are layer around.

Note: you may make the mitts smaller or lengthy below. Simply crochet shell lines if you

Need them longer, less if you like them smaller.

ch 3.

In next power, ch 1, layer in 4 occasions, sl st directly into of ch. 3. (You've overlooked

one layer and 2 dcs to help make the flash starting.)

Strip 9: Sl st in subsequent dc & ch 1 room, plead shell, (dc in next electricity, shell in next shell) about,

Closing DC-in ch 1 between covers, sl st in top of starting ch 3. (You Have added one dc

Back to your strip.)

Place in stops, secure down, appreciate!

All Grown Up Arm Warmers

US- 5.5mm catch, I

Worsted weight wool, roughly 185 meters all of two shades (Caron Simply Gentle in Dark and Grey Heather revealed)

Measure: 13 dc = 4″ broad (when operating lines); 12 sc = 3″ (period of cuff)

Arm/Hand Cuff:

Using Color A and making an 8″ butt, ch 13. Change.

Strip 1: Employed In sc within the ch in the catch BLO, and each ch. Ch 1. was created by 12 sc

Strip 2 – 32(36): Sc in BLO equally across Ch 1 and change. 12 sc

Strip 33(37): Change to function in to the aspect of the cuff, looping the item right into a ribbed cuff, so the first and last line fulfill. Ch 1 in to the aspect of each strip and 1st strip as shown below. Don't join. 32(36) sc

Lines Area:

Round 1: Place the catch in to the 1st street of Strip 33(37), hey with Shade W, and create sl st to participate. Ch 2. [Bpdc in 2 sts, then] 8(9) situations. Join with sl ch and st 2. 24(27) sts

Round 2: [DC-In 6(7) sts, then dc2tog] three times. Join with sl ch and st 2. 21(24) sts

Round 3: [DC-In 8(10) sts dc2tog] twice. Small-size only: DC-in last street. Don't join. 19(22) sts

Round 4: With Shade A, join the prior strip having a sl st's finish. Join with sl ch and st 2. 19(22) sts

Round 5: DC-In 1st st. (large-size only: 2 DC-in the following street.) Dc each st. DC - 2 in last street. Join with sl ch and st 2. 20(24) sts

Round 6: DC-In each street around. Don't join. 20(24) sts

Round 7: With Color W, join the prior strip having a sl st's finish. Join with sl ch and st 2. 20(24) sts

Round 8: DC-In the first st 2 DC-in the following st. Dc-in sts 2 DC-in st, to final st. Join with sl ch and st 2. 22(26) sts

Round 9: DC-In the first st 2 DC-in the following st. Dc-in sts 2 DC-in st, to final st. Don't join. 24(28) sts

Round 10: With Shade A, join the prior strip having a sl st's finish. Join with sl ch and st 2. 24(28) sts

Round 11: DC-In the first st 2 DC-in the following st. Dc-in sts 2 DC-in st, to final st. Join with sl ch and st 2. 26(30) sts

Round 12: DC-In the first st 2 DC-in the following st. Dc-in sts 2 DC-in st, to final st. Don't join. 28(32) sts

Round 13: crochet arm socks that are free patterneach e around. Join with sl ch and st 2. 28(32) sts

Round 14: DC-In the first st 2 DC-in the following st. Dc-in sts 2 DC-in st, to final st. Join with sl ch and st 2. 30(34) sts

Round 15: DC-In the first st 2 DC-in the following st. Dc-in sts 2 DC-in st, to final st. Don't join. 32(36) sts Split Shade W, making an extended enough butt to incorporate in later.

One Skein Fingerless

US – M 9.0 mm catch, /D

80 yds (2.5 oz) cumbersome weight wool (a little less than 1 skein Lion Brand Distinctive, Grapevine found)

Repeat from. Join having a sl st towards the fpdc. (18 sts)

Ch 1, round 4: CSDC, DC-in the following st, ch 1 *Dc within the next 2 sts, miss 1 st. Repeat from. Join having a sl st towards the CSDC.

Round 5: CSDC, miss the next street, operating within the ch 1 in the prior round, function 2 dc sts in to the overlooked st of the strip below the prior strip (Round 3). *Dc within the next st, miss the st, operating the ch 1 within in the prior round, function 2 dc sts below the prior strip in to the overlooked st of the row. Repeat from. Join having a sl st towards the CSDC. (18 sts)

Round 6: the next street, skips. Repeat until 1 st stays from *, DC-in the final street. Join having a sl st towards the CSDC.

Round 7: CSDC, operating in the prior round within the ch 1, function 2 dc sts in to the overlooked street of the row below the prior strip. *Skip the following st, DC-in the following st, operating the ch 1 within in the prior round, function 2 dc sts below the prior strip in to the overlooked st of the row. From * until 1 st repeat stays, miss the last street. Join having a sl st towards the CSDC. (18 sts)

Round 8 – 9: Repeat Models 4 – 5.

Round 10: (Making the thumb-hole.) CSDC, ch 1, miss the next st, DC-in the following 2 sts, ch 1, miss the next st, DC-in the following 3 sts, ch 2, skip 2 sts, DC-in the following 3 sts, ch 1, miss the next st, DC-in the following 2 sts, ch 1, miss the next st, DC-in the final st. Join having a sl st towards the CSDC.

Round 11: CSDC, operating in the prior round within the ch 1, function 2 dc sts below the prior strip in to the overlooked st of the row, miss the st, DC-in the following st. Join having a sl st towards the CSDC. (15 sts)

Round 12: Repeat Round 2, closing having a fpdc within the last street. Utilize smooth and split string join to complete off.

Chapter 3 – 2 Great and new patterns!

Oh my gosh Gloves

Materials:

50 gr of DK weight yarn, in Main Colour (MC);

50 gr of DK weight string, in Supporting Shade (CC);

(100 gr of DK weight string if you are going for the single color option);

Hook.

Recommendations (x2):

Cuff:

Chain 30, with MC, join to make a circle, being careful never to twist the sequence.

Hdc in each sequence across, Row 1: Chain 2, slip-stitch for the Round 2 initially to hitch;

Rows 2-12: Round 2, hdc in each street across, slip-stitch towards the string 2 initially to participate (this can be wherever you select the length of time you would like your cuff; less lines suggests a quicker cuff, more rows a longer one);

Break wool off.

Hand:

Row 14: Sequence 1, sc within the same st, *5 DC-in ch 3 room, miss 1 st, sc in subsequent st* (middle st of the previous row), replicate from * to * until the stop, slip-stitch to join;

Row 15: slip-stitch to minute power of cluster, sequence 1, sc inside the same street, 2 sc, *ch 3, 3 sc at the center dcs of cluster from previous row*, replicate from * to * before conclusion, slip stitch to join;

Strip 16: Slip stitch to second sc, string 1, sc inside the same st, *5 dc in ch 3 area, miss 1 st, sc in following st* (middle st of the previous row), repeat from * to * before stop, slip stitch to join;

Strip 17: Repeat row 15;

Strip 18: Repeat row 16;

Strip 19: Repeat line 15;

Line 20: Repeat row 16;

Line 21: Slip stitch to minute dc of cluster, Round 1, sc in the same street, 2 sc, sequence 3, skip one cluster, 3 sc in the middle dcs of second cluster from previous strip, *chain 3, 3 sc at the center dcs of second cluster from prior row* repeat from * to * until the conclusion, slip stitch to hitch;

Strip 22: Repeat line 16;

Line 23: Repeat line 15;

Row 24: Repeat row 16.

Butterfly Stitch Fingerless Gloves

Snare: 5.5 mm snare/I snare

YARN: not exactly a skein of Worsted weight yarn – US 4 utilize or AU 10 handle yarn.

100 grams/3.5. oz

240 meters/262 yards

Line 1

Sc in second ch from snare. *sl st in next fasten, ch 3 and skirt a line and sl st into next, sc in next stitch* Repeat for column. sc in last st. (sc, sl st, ch 3, sk a st, sl st) at end, ch 1 and turn

Line 2

Sc in first st, * BFS 4 times in the ch 3 space from past line then sl st into the sc * Repeat til end of column.

Sl st into line BEFORE the last line, leaving the last line of the line. Presently utilizing this last join of the column, get the opposite side of the line and adjust it. sl st sew utilizing the last join of the column and it's equivalent on the other tip as appeared in picture 2.

Sl st twice to sew and frame a ring. Ch 1

Rounds 3 and 4

SC into all sts around (25 sts) ensure you end the rounds with 25 lines, if you need to diminish once then do as such.

Rounds 5 – 16 (12 rounds)

BFS utilizing your initial 2 sts (on the grounds that the BFS/Butterfly Stitch takes 2 fastens to make) and Place line marker here. Proceed with the round and when you get to the end, do the first part of the Butterfly line in the last line of the round and complete the butterfly join utilizing that long first line of the round.

Work your BFS utilizing the wings of the butterflies from last column. Starting in one wing and completing the join in the following such as demonstrated as follows. Keep stitching in the winding round for an aggregate of 12 rounds. NOTE: Always tally your rounds from the left half of your marker. (I for one number more than two lines to one side of my marker, then begin checking my columns up from that point til I tally 10 lines and my snare is toward the start of the line to begin Round 17, then I begin my thumb.)

Round 1 of thumb

sl into the following fasten and ch 6, skirt 4 sts and sl st in the fifth. At that point proceed with your BFS's as ordinary until you achieve thumb opening once more. Bear in mind to BFS in the area just before the thumb.

Round 2

Work 3 BFS's into the ch 6 space and sl st into the following st. Proceed with your BFS's as ordinary. (picture just shows 2 BFS's yet 3 works better!)

Round 3

MARK THIS STITCH BEFORE THE THUMB and keep on working your BFS's over the thumb as typical. Presently you might see you have 2 join after the thumb that are not a past BFS. This is a direct result of the sl sts you did the last two rounds. So utilizing these 2 fastens, work a BFS as ordinary and afterward proceed with the round with BFS's as typical until you achieve your marker once more.

Rounds 4 and 5

Work your BFS's as ordinary until you achieve your marker.

Chapter 4 – The Ideas Behind Crochet Patterns

Each year the designs change, yet the hues are dependably on the same cycles. Spring and summer calls for splendid and new hues while harvest time and winter ordinarily shouts out for tans and blacks and every single darker tone.

With new molds, certain extras change that blast into new rages. One of these new rages is knit designs. Keep in mind the first run through around stitch examples were only for liners and teapot covers.

Disregard the old school designs for blinds, or place settings and even liners. Design is about creative energy and having the capacity to look great and set a pattern. Thusly is shoddy and simple, it permits straightforward examples to be changed into extraordinary looks

Thoughts for a straightforward knit example could be flawless as some itemizing on a plain match of pants, to give a free and creative look that nobody else has. Utilizing the hues as a part of style, a knit example could make an awesome, lovely tote that you can change with the seasons. Why not complete off the outfit by knitting a blossom onto a coat to give that last detail.

Examples might come in diverse sizes and shapes, contingent upon what you need to utilize them for. In some cases the sew examples will be as creatures or banners. For the more enthusiastic amongst us, hues can be coordinated with the yarn for the sought impact.

If you need sew designs there are such a large number of out there, in magazines and on the web. There are a great many outlines accessible, however by utilizing your own creative energy you will go over incredible one of a kind examples that nobody else has.

Search with the expectation of complimentary blessings with eBook buys and connections to examples that could likewise be of enthusiasm to the beginner or experienced crocheter.

It's not just ladies who can profit by stitch designs, in extreme times there are numerous outlines for youngsters' garments and plans for men also. Why not individualize yourself by utilizing an example for caps, gloves and scarves for the winter and light coats in the mid year? Men can utilize designs for patches on coat arms or beginning another pattern on bicycle coats and knocking down some pins shirts for instance.

There are vintage designs accessible for ladies as scarves, capes and coats for free mold in the colder months.

Making a sew example can be entirely simple if you have fundamental information of knitting and the lines that make distinctive examples. After that all that is expected to finish the thing is the yarn and revise size snare for the outline you need to depict.

To make your own particular sew design it might be a smart thought to coax it out on paper first. Once the design is finished you can take the example to a nearby yarn look for exhortation on the perfect yarn and consummate hues. Ensure you get the right weight of yarn as this will figure out whether the thing is expandable or not.

If you are new to stitch, if merits attempting some effectively finished examples before attempting your own, to figure out the yarn thickness and weight, before moving onto more propelled plans and making designs for yourself.

The most profitable approach to learn design systems are through books and can be found on the web at great costs and here and there even free!

These sources demonstrate the plans and lines included and how to do it so anybody can get on with a little practice.

There are still a lot of examples to be found in philanthropy shops and at shopping centers. Claim to fame shops ordinarily have a decent gathering of outlines. Have a go at going into the shop and grabbing a made piece to feel the weight and composition before obtaining the example. This will help you when you return home and begin knitting yourself.

Keep in mind those liners and place settings from prior? Why not transform those into a style proclamation? These can be utilized for regular wear and transformed into a wide range of style things; simply utilize your creative energy! Why purchase it from the shops when you can do it without anyone's help without leaving your home, and for a large portion of the cost at home?

Yes, I'm not imagining that utilizing stitch designs and taking in another leisure activity is brisk and simple, yet all your diligent work will pay off when you are complimented on your individual style. Nobody else will ever have the same look, regardless of the possibility that they utilize the same example as every piece is absolutely special. With a little creative ability and capable hands the open doors for style are interminable!

Stitch designs and plans don't generally need to be fresh out of the box new, Vintage designs have as of late returned into style and can be utilized for any season utilizing lighter yarn and shading for the late spring and not overlooking darker and heavier yarns for the winter. That said why should I say when and how you ought to wear your sewed things?

Conclusion

Winters are as of now here and Indian ladies are going all out with their sewing needles. They weave pullovers, scarves, gloves and what not with yarn and a couple of needles. Weaving woolen garments is more like a custom amongst Indian ladies and a considerable lot of them are capable at it. Weaving is a basic piece of Indian culture and nothing else can assume its position. Yet, if you wish to improve your expertise set by taking in another type of craftsmanship then stitch is the best decision.

Knit

Knit is a procedure wherein a fabric is made utilizing string and a sew snare. Sew is all that much like sewing with the exception of that the previous uses one needle rather than two. At first, it might be hard to make a fabric utilizing a solitary needle however with little practice you will have the capacity to learn sewing. Alongside honing this new type of sewing, you have to comprehend the key contrasts between customary sewing and knitting. Thusly, the learning procedure would turn out to be speedier.

Contrasts between Crocheting and Knitting

1. In stitch, we utilize stand out knit snare. Despite what might be expected, weaving requires two needles at one time.

2. Following stand out snare is utilized as a part of knit, it has one and only live join on the snare. Be that as it may, amid sewing there can be more than one live join on the needle.

3. With a sew snare, it is less demanding to make round or barrel shaped examples. In any case, this is not the situation with sewing. To make roundabout or tube shaped examples in sewing, the individual might require extraordinary sort of weaving needles, arranged knit snare set and extras

4. The measure of yarn required in sew is for the most part more than weaving. Before you begin rehearsing any of the structures, ensure that you have enough

measure of yarn in stock. Furthermore, if you are running shy of yarn or whatever other weaving supply then request it effortlessly through Internet.

5. You can make three-dimensional examples effortlessly with stitch snares as new snares are done autonomously.

Things Needed for Crocheting

At this point you probably comprehended the fundamental contrasts in the middle of sewing and sewing. Presently, if you wish to realize this new fine art then you should have the fundamental things. For sewing, the first thing you need is yarn. The string ought to be of good quality so that the final item looks lovely. Aside from yarn, you should purchase a few sew snares.

FREE Bonus Reminder

If you have not grabbed it yet, please go ahead and download your special bonus report *"DIY Projects. 13 Useful & Easy To Make DIY Projects To Save Money & Improve Your Home!"*
Simply Click the Button Below

OR Go to **This Page**
http://diyhomecraft.com/free

BONUS #2: More Free Books
Do you want to receive more Free Books?
We have a mailing list where we send out our new Books when they go free on Kindle. Click on the link below to sign up for Free Book Promotions.
=> Sign Up for Free Book Promotions <=

OR Go to this URL
http://zbit.ly/1WBb1Ek

Printed in the USA
CPSIA information can be obtained
at www.ICGtesting.com
LVHW051213281123
765067LV00005B/666

9 781542 574297